Original title:
Under the Green Glow

Copyright © 2025 Creative Arts Management OÜ
All rights reserved.

Author: Harris Montgomery
ISBN HARDBACK: 978-1-80581-923-3
ISBN PAPERBACK: 978-1-80581-450-4
ISBN EBOOK: 978-1-80581-923-3

Ethereal Light and Lush Delight

In a forest of giggles, the leaves dance round,
When a squirrel drops acorns, it makes a loud sound.
The fairies are laughing, wearing shoes of moss,
With hats made of petals, they're never at loss.

The sun dips down low, casting shadows so funny,
While rabbits throw parties, with snacks like honey.
A frog in a top hat croaks jokes from a log,
While butterflies chase each other—just a big smog.

Twilight in the Emerald Wood

As twilight descends, the trees stretch and yawn,
A raccoon on a branch sings a nocturnal brawn.
With the stars blinking brightly, they join in the song,
The critters all chuckle, 'What's taking so long?'

A fox with a beard looks quite dapper and bold,
His wit is sharp; watch out for tricks that unfold.
A glow-worm exhibits his luminescent flair,
And the owls debate who's got the best hair.

The Poetry of Foliage

In a canopy world of lush leafy verse,
Chirping birds share puns—oh, it's wonderfully terse.
Each branch whispers secrets, a delightful jest,
While worms in bow ties declare, 'We're the best!'

With foliage friends, the laughter won't cease,
The bushes all giggle, promising peace.
A mushroom recites rhymes that leave us all grinning,
While the grasses sway softly, their own dance beginning.

Emerald Echoes

Echoes of laughter ripple through the air,
As critters play tag without a single care.
A hedgehog in spectacles reads poetry loud,
While mushrooms applaud, forming a funky crowd.

Each rustle of leaves holds a chorus of cheer,
With dragonflies zipping like they're in high gear.
A bear in pajamas brings forth a parade,
As they shimmy in style, entirely unafraid.

Dappled Dreams

In the forest's quirky dance,
Frogs wear hats and squirrels prance.
Mushrooms giggle, hiding well,
While owls play chess in twilight's spell.

Breezes tell mischief in the air,
Laughter echoes, weeds declare.
A leafy caper, oh what a sight,
Critters gathering for the night!

Green Serenity

Blades of grass, a tickle spree,
Worms are wriggling, wild and free.
A tree with glasses reads a tale,
As raindrops laugh and sunbeams sail.

Mossy stones play hide and seek,
While bees compose a buzzing streak.
Nature's choir in merry tune,
Singing softly to the moon!

The Light Between the Leaves

Amidst the branches, shadows sway,
A rabbit's dance, hip-hop ballet.
Sunbeams peek, a game of tag,
While flowers sway their petals brag.

Butterflies wear ridiculous shoes,
Collecting pollen, spreading news.
Under the canopy, giggles arise,
As fireflies wear their tiny ties.

A Green Mosaic

Caterpillars host a fancy feast,
With lettuce leaves, they're quite the beast.
Painted rocks gossip with old roots,
And ladybugs wear their polka suits.

The garden party never ends,
Where every weed is best of friends.
A riot of colors, nature's role,
In this zany, green, cheerful stroll.

The Enchantment of Shaded Paths

In a forest quite lively, trees dance with glee,
Squirrels now attempting a synchronized spree.
With acorns a-flying, they trip and they fall,
Laughing together, they bounce like a ball.

A rabbit in glasses, contemplating a joke,
Says, "What did the tree say to the oak?"
No answer, just giggles, as leaves sway so bright,
In this chatty green place, all worries take flight.

Illuminated Ferns

Ferns flicker their fronds like they're waving hello,
While mushrooms are knitting, there's much to bestow.
A snail with a hat claims he's late for a race,
While hedgehogs roll by, sporting smiles on their face.

A glowworm declares it's time for a dance,
While crickets all chirp, giving silence a chance.
The moon starts to giggle, spilling light on the ground,
With laughter of critters, a night fairytale found.

Green Serenade

In a bouncy bush band, the frogs sing along,
Their croaks become melodies, silly but strong.
While badgers are woofing in harmony tact,
And fireflies flash out the rhythm, intact.

Two foxes in tweed, they're twirling with grace,
In footwear of daisies, they waltz in this space.
Each so-called misstep brings giggles anew,
As the night plays its symphony, just for the crew.

A Glint in the Woodland

With a wink from the willows, secrets unfold,
Each rabbit, a joker, amidst stories told.
An owl cracks a pun that just never gets old,
While the breeze carries laughter, like treasures of gold.

In the midst of the glimmer, a wise turtle sings,
"I've found the best shade, where the laughter springs!"
And as critters all gather to bask in the cheer,
The woodland keeps giggling, year after year.

Emerald Dreams

In a field full of beans, oh so bright,
The cows dance like it's a wild flight.
Chasing butterflies with a glee,
They trip and tumble, just like me!

Fairies giggle, hiding behind trees,
While squirrels shake their fuzzy knees.
A rabbit hops, thinking he's grand,
But lands in a puddle – oh, isn't life planned?

The Radiance of Leaves

The leaves are blushing, oh what a sight,
Waving hello in the soft light.
A chipmunk struts, adjusts his bow tie,
Says with flair, 'I'm a dapper guy!'

The sun plays hide and seek, so sly,
While ants march on like they're in the sky.
A toadstool rises, 'Join my parade!'
As laughter bursts from the woodland shade.

Beneath the Forest's Light

A sloth hangs low, what a slow fright,
Grumbling, 'Is it day, or is it night?'
The mushrooms giggle, they've seen it all,
As a hedgehog slips and starts to sprawl.

The fireflies dance, all dressed in style,
One trips over, makes us all smile.
They twinkle and flicker, what's that ruckus?
Just lightning bugs in a grand circus.

Enchanted Glade

In the glade where whispers roam free,
A deer checks her hair, 'Oh look at me!'
Her friends chuckle, 'What a grand show!'
But trip on roots, 'Who put them low?'

Mushrooms sit round, tea time's begun,
With acorn hats, they frolic and run.
A wise old owl with a monocle stares,
'What's the fuss? Who cares about flares?'

A Dance of Light and Leaves

In a forest, leaves prance and sway,
Chasing shadows, they frolic and play.
Sunbeams twirl with a giggle and spin,
Whispers of mischief where laughter begins.

Squirrels in caps, dance on a beam,
Chasing their tails, a slapstick scene.
All in the glow of a bright leafy haze,
Nature's own stage for whimsical plays.

The breeze blows a tune, cheeky and bold,
Tickling the branches as stories unfold.
With every step, they make the trees laugh,
In this green-lit jig, it's a playful gaffe.

Here in the woods, joy takes its flight,
In the dappled glow, everything's bright.
Under the sun's chuckle, we sway in delight,
A dance of pure fun in the warm afternoon light.

The Mystique of Chlorophyll Dreams

In dreams of green, where the oddities grow,
A cabbage in top hat steals quite the show.
It waltzes with weeds, in a top-secret scheme,
Together they plot, in chlorophyll dreams.

A dandy old root gives a deep, hearty laugh,
While twirling furiously, it's quite the gaffe.
The mushrooms all giggle, their caps in a spin,
As pickle jars roll; let the odd games begin!

A dancing tomato, with swagger and style,
Takes the stage solo, strutting a mile.
But the peas in their pods, oh, they're quite the jest,
In a chorus of chuckles, they laugh at the rest.

In this glimmering world, joy isn't far,
With every green petal, a whimsical star.
So hold onto your hats as you join in the schemes,
For life is a laugh in the land of green dreams.

Serpents of Light on a Fern-Laden Floor

Snakes of sunshine slither through leaves,
Making light wiggle, oh what a tease!
Ferns stand guard, like fluffy green knights,
While beams of laughter take fanciful flights.

The mushrooms all whistle, a jolly old tune,
As the sun beams giggle and dance with the moon.
In this playful maze, the shadows all roam,
They twirl and they swerve like they're far from home.

A caterpillar sings in a fashionable hat,
Dancing to rhythms where silliness sat.
With each little jolt, the leaves shake and quake,
As winks from the sun spin their playful wake.

Nature's own circus, no room for despair,
Underneath branches that tickle the air.
The serpents of light, they giggle and gleam,
In this fern-laden floor, it's a hilarious dream.

Serenity in the Green Twilight

In the twilight where shadows don a grin,
Grassy knolls giggle as night creeps in.
Whispers of humor float soft on the breeze,
Napping critters chuckle beneath snoring trees.

A wise old owl, in spectacles round,
Spends his night sharing tales with the ground.
With a flick of his wings, he sends stars in glee,
And the crickets keep time, a tune for the trees.

The breeze plays a prank, rustling through hair,
Leaves leap with laughter, without any care.
Frogs croak rhymes in curious tongue,
Celebrating the dusk where hilarity's sprung.

As moonlight spills shimmer across the floor,
The earth hums a laughter, an echoing roar.
In this serene space, where the chuckles ignite,
We all share a smile, in the green twilight.

Beneath the Emerald Canopy

Squirrels play poker, bets on acorns,
While birds sing ballads of ancient horns.
Frogs become dancers, jumping with glee,
In a waltz with the breezes, oh so free.

Mice wear top hats, sipping on dew,
Debating the weather, what else to do?
Rabbits declare a race, tails in the air,
As turtles just chuckle, taking their care.

Whispers of Verdant Light

Ants in a line, organizing a feast,
Chewing on crumbs, they've conquered the least.
They wave to the ladybug passing by,
While bees trade gossip, oh my, oh my!

The leaves are whispering secrets so bold,
Tales of the creatures, both young and old.
A chameleon's grinning, blending with ease,
Saying, "You'll never catch me, just try, if you please!"

Shadows in the Leafy Embrace

A snail writes sonnets, longing for speed,
While grasshoppers giggle at his little deed.
The shadows are dancing, throwing a ball,
Inviting all critters—come one, come all!

Raccoons in tuxedos with masks on their eyes,
Planning a heist under luminous skies.
Chasing moonbeams, they trip and they roll,
Tickling the roots, oh, that's their goal!

The Luminance of Nature's Veil

Fireflies flicker, fashioning bling,
Competing for style, oh what a fling!
The elder tree chuckles, gnarled and wise,
"Who needs a gyro when you've got these guys?"

Fluttering fairies, mischief in flight,
Sneaking on gnomes who nap day and night.
With twinkling giggles, they toss leafy hats,
A showdown ensues between dogs and the cats.

Green Haven's Soliloquy

In the garden, gnomes converse,
With plants that jest, it's quite diverse.
One claims to grow the biggest bean,
While flowers giggle, unseen, unseen.

A snail on stilts boasts of his speed,
While daisies laugh, "You'll never lead!"
The toads throw parties, frogs in tow,
All in a frenzy to steal the show.

Butterflies argue who flits best,
While worms deploy their dirt-digging quest.
A hedgehog rolls in laughter loud,
His quills a crown, he feels so proud.

In this haven where chaos reigns,
Nature's humor, she can't contain.
Join the fun, leave worries behind,
In this whimsical world, joy you'll find.

Murmurs of Nature's Light

The crickets chirp their clever puns,
While fireflies dance, a show for fun.
A squirrel slips, his acorn flies,
And the woods erupt with little sighs.

The wind whispers jokes through swaying trees,
As raccoons plan their midnight tease.
A wise old owl hoots out a cheer,
His jokes are corny, but we all hear.

Roses blush at the humor spun,
While daisies nod, their tails all done.
In this chat where nature winks,
The laughter flows like gentle streams.

So come, join in the playful jest,
With splashes of light, it's pure zest.
In this realm of giggles and cheer,
The joys of nature are always near.

Journey Through the Leafy Veil

Through leafy paths where shadows play,
A turtle claims he's had a say.
The mushrooms grumble, "We grow better!"
While ferns compete in a silly feta.

The path's alive with chittering chat,
A raccoon's stuck, oh what of that!
He fashion-tips his spotted coat,
While all the flora just gloat and gloat.

A breeze comes through, a playful gust,
Tickling leaves, in nature we trust.
The owls throw feathers, feathery flings,
And nature's chorus merrily sings.

In this journey where pranks unfold,
Each leaf a story, bright and bold.
So stroll along, let laughter prevail,
And find the fun in the leafy veil.

Lush Light in the Twilight Wood

In twilight wood, the shadows dance,
Where rabbits plot their nighttime prance.
A hedgehog grins, his snout all spry,
While nighttime stars begin to fly.

The owls exchange their nightly chime,
With jokes that stretch beyond all time.
The bushes sway in fits of glee,
As twilight's sparkles set them free.

A wise old tree shares tales so tall,
Of a spider's web that caught them all.
While shadows chuckle, hidden from sight,
In this lush light where giggles ignite.

So wander forth, with joy in heart,
In this wood where laughter's an art.
Embrace the night, join in their cheer,
In twilight's glow, all fun is near.

A Palette of Silhouettes

In the forest, trees wear coats,
Dancin' squirrels, they take the votes.
Colors splash as shadows blend,
As branches twist and branches bend.

A rabbit twerks, he's got some flair,
While birds all laugh without a care.
The mushrooms giggle, what a sight,
As fireflies join in the night.

A deer steps in, with style so grand,
Winks at a bug, they form a band.
The paint drips down from skies so vast,
Art's alive here, running fast!

So grab your brush, let's paint away,
In this lively, leafy ballet.
With twinkling stars and leafy glow,
A masterpiece, with nature's flow.

The Whispering Boughs

Whispers hum from branches high,
Trees gossip as the breezes sigh.
A squirrel drops an acorn ball,
He swears it's true, once made him tall.

Leaves gossip in a crackling tone,
What's the latest? Who's alone?
The bushes rustle, sharing jokes,
While hedgehogs laugh at their own pokes.

A butterfly swoops, all aglow,
Saying, 'Hey, where'd you get that bow?'
The mushrooms snicker, in a line,
"Fashion tips? Do they serve wine?"

So join the chatter, come take a peek,
In a forest that's quirky, fun and unique.
Nature's prattle, it makes us grin,
In this cozy nook, let the laughter begin.

Veils of Light in the Wild

Sunbeams tickle through the trees,
Light drips down like warm, sweet peas.
A fox prances, wears a mask,
Pretending to be some cool, sly task.

The shadows dance, a playful game,
"Who's the best at hide-and-seek?" they claim.
A raccoon trips, he missed a cue,
Lands in a patch, calls it his 'venue'.

The fireflies twirl in glowing rounds,
As laughter echoes through the grounds.
"Catch me if you can!" they flicker and dart,
While candles of light steal the heart.

Ah, the magic, it sparkles bright,
With giggles woven in the night.
Nature stages a comical show,
In beams that shimmer with a gentle glow.

Rhythms of the Emerald Forest

The clumsy bear forgets his beat,
Trips over roots, man, what a feat!
Frogs leap by, they sing at last,
"Keep it down! You're a real outcast!"

A woodpecker's tap is the drum's loud call,
"Who's got the moves? C'mon, let's ball!"
The crickets chirp with a funky tone,
While vines twist and groove like they own the zone.

A raccoon struts with a stylish flair,
Challenging foxes to a dance in pairs.
Laughter sounds like a forest song,
As creatures join in, where they belong.

So grab a partner, embrace the fun,
In this emerald haven, there's room for everyone.
With rhythms alive, let your spirit soar,
In the wild, we're forever more.

Reflections in a Leafy Oasis

In a jungle of dreams and rhymes,
Frogs wear hats and dance in times.
Squirrels sip tea with a twist of lime,
While birds recite their bestest chimes.

Turtles play checkers on lily pads,
Counting each move with grins and jads.
A bubble of laughter pops in the air,
As insects debate who's had the best flair.

A rabbit juggles acorns with ease,
While ants applaud and shimmy their knees.
The whole scene feels like a whimsical show,
In this leafy oasis, where hilarity flows.

With giggles and glee, the sunlight streams,
In this park of delights and silly dreams.
Every moment's a jest, every shadow a friend,
Wonders unfold, where fun knows no end.

Whimsy Beneath the Trees

Beneath the branches where shadows play,
Dancing mushrooms join the fray.
A raccoon in spectacles reads a book,
While wise old owls give knowing looks.

The rabbits perform, a tap dance show,
While chipmunks cheer from their acorn row.
A snail on a skateboard zooms right by,
Underneath a low-flying butterfly.

A chorus of frogs sing out in tune,
As the sun dips low and sings to the moon.
Every leaf sways to the rhythm of glee,
In a world of whimsy beneath the trees.

So grab your hat and join the scene,
Where every corner hides something keen.
Laughter surrounds like a breeze in the air,
In this playful realm, there's joy everywhere.

The Emerald Lullaby

In the meadow where giggles grow,
A sprightly breeze begins to blow.
Puppy dogs leap with boundless cheer,
While butterflies sip on nectar dear.

The grasshoppers host a musical night,
Playing tall tales till morning light.
Crickets with charm pull a fun little trick,
As fireflies dance with a magical flick.

Bubbles float by on a whimsy ride,
Soft pillows of clouds keep dreams inside.
The sun winks down with a twinkly eye,
As the world hums softly a lullaby.

So let's sway with joy till the stars take their place,
In this emerald dream, with a smile on our face.
Every moment a treasure, a sparkle, a thing,
In the sweetest embrace that laughter can bring.

Moonlight Kisses Green

In the quiet of night, where giggles blend,
Wise old cats are the best of friends.
With shadows as partners in a silly dance,
They prance and they twirl, not leaving to chance.

Mice in tuxedos tap out a beat,
While the flowers join in with twinkling feet.
Beneath the moon's glow, the fun never wanes,
As butterflies laugh in their shimmering chains.

The night blooms bright with whimsical glee,
Every creature's a part of this jubilee.
As stars wink brightly and fireflies twirl,
This moonlit magic begins to unfurl.

With laughter as soft as a cozy quilt,
In the velvety twilight, joy is built.
So join in the chorus of night's lovely dream,
Where moonlight kisses every fun little beam.

Serenade of the Forest Shadows

In the woods where crickets sing,
A squirrel's dance, a silly fling,
The owls wear spectacles, oh so bright,
They read the news by moon's soft light.

Beneath a tree, a raccoon grins,
He's found a stash of jelly beans,
With froggy friends on lily pads,
They throw a party, isn't that mad?

A badger tries to juggle pine,
While hedgehogs cheer with mugs of brine,
The mushrooms giggle, shake, and sway,
Join in the fun, come out and play!

So join the dance, don't be a stoop,
In leafy lanes, you'll find the troop,
With silly songs and laughter loud,
In this green realm, come be unbowed!

The Lure of the Glade

A bunny wearing shoes so neat,
Places bets on dancing feet,
His carrot chips, they rattle and roll,
As chipmunks spin in a rock 'n' roll.

The grass too tall for ants to climb,
They've formed a band, it's quite sublime,
With leaf guitars, they strum away,
A concert held beneath the sway.

Frogs with hats sing silly tunes,
Beneath the glow of silver moons,
They croak and hop, a merry sight,
Their toes a-tappin', what a fright!

Join this crowd, don't miss the fun,
Where nature's mischief never's done,
In leafy glades, where laughter streams,
The forest lives in wildest dreams.

In the Heart of Verdant Dreams

A gnome in rainboots splashes around,
While pixies giggle at the sound,
He tries to catch a flying leaf,
But tumbles down, oh what a grief!

A turtle wears a roller hat,
Zooms past saying, "Not too flat!"
While ladybugs play hopscotch there,
Beneath the trees, without a care.

The trees all whisper, "What a show!"
As garden gnomes practice their glow,
With juggling acts and silly poses,
They bring to life the forest's roses.

Here in this space of laughter's way,
Where fireflies dance on bright display,
Join the fun, the quirky schemes,
In the heart of these vibrant dreams!

Fables of Glimmering Green

Once there was a cat so spry,
He claimed to speak with clouds on high,
A mouse retorted, "Hold your fluff,
You're more of a couch potato, tough!"

The ants all told their tall tales fast,
Of treasures found and flags amassed,
Yet someone sneezed, they all did scatter,
And lost their prize, oh such a clatter!

A frog in slippers plays all day,
Hopping along on his leafy way,
With puddles big enough to splash,
He's drawn quite a crowd to the bash!

So gather 'round for stories keen,
Of creatures cheeky and verdant green,
For life is strange and full of glee,
In these fables of mystery!

Emerald Tango

In the garden, boots a swing,
To the rhythm, frogs are king.
The daisies giggle, oh so bright,
While moonbeams join the quirky night.

Squirrels twist and twirl with glee,
The raccoons shout, "Join the spree!"
With a hearty laugh, the leaves reply,
Beneath the stars, all spirits fly.

A dancer clad in leafy green,
Spins 'round, looking quite the scene.
The wise old owl hoots a tune,
As fireflies flicker, oh what a boon!

Crickets chirp in little shoes,
While snails serve up the party brews.
With nature's jesters all around,
In leafy joy, our laughs abound.

Dance of the Moonlit Foliage

Beneath the glow of silvery light,
Plants conspire for a wild night.
Mossy capes and stems so spry,
Join the jig, oh me, oh my!

A bashful vine begins to sway,
While owls chuckle, come what may.
With every leaf, a giggle grows,
As petals point their tiny toes.

The sneaky beetles pass the hat,
While fireflies are where it's at.
A concert screams through buzzing sounds,
As laughter weaves through tangled grounds.

And when the sun peeks out to see,
The joyous crew with glee and spree,
They'll try to dance, but fall instead,
All tangled joy, from toes to head.

Shadows of Verdant Splendor

In leafy shrouds, the laughter hides,
Where jokesters in the shade reside.
A twig's a wand, a leaf's a hat,
As shadows prance in chatter chat.

The ferns debate who jumps the best,
While robins cheer, a daring quest.
With snickers rolled from every bough,
Each whispered joke is celebrated now.

Lizards shimmy, finding mates,
While honeysuckles share the fates.
In this leafy carnival they hold,
Laughter's worth more than any gold.

But should a breeze come hastily,
The boundless giggle floats so free.
As echoes dance through tangled trees,
The fun defies all boundaries!

Glimmers Among the Vines

Where the glow meets creeping vines,
A party starts, oh how it shines!
Where bees serve sweets, not a care,
And whispers float in the sweet air.

With cheeky winks that nature sends,
Squirrels dress up to play pretend.
The daisies join, with petals wide,
As laughter resonates like the tide.

Each beetle boasts about their capes,
While thrushes sing in funny shapes.
The wind tickles leaves, a playful tease,
As creatures sway with enjoyable ease.

When twilight falls, the giggles rise,
To serenade the starry skies.
The night's a stage where the jokes are prime,
In glimmers bright, it's silly time!

Celestial Beams through the Forest's Breath

In the forest, beams do creep,
Chasing critters from their sleep.
A raccoon winks, a skunk holds still,
Laughing leaves, with twinkling will.

Bats in capes do swoop and glide,
While owls hoot, they laugh and hide.
Stars above in jest do tease,
As squirrels dance among the trees.

Treetops Bathed in Bioluminescence

A glowworm held a party bright,
Inviting bugs to dance all night.
Fireflies flit with sparkly flair,
Beneath the glow, the world's a fair!

Twirling leaves in colors bold,
Echo tales of mischief told.
The frogs croak out a silly tune,
While crickets fiddle just beneath the moon.

The Viridian Veil of Secrecy

Behind the ferns, a sneaky pair,
A hedgehog and a cat so rare.
They plot to steal a honey jar,
But end up stuck, oh how bizarre!

The trees, they giggle, swaying tall,
As critters stumble, rise, and fall.
In whispers light, the secrets flow,
But no one knows where trouble's go.

Dreaming in the Shade of Giants

Beneath the branches, dreams take flight,
A snail claims victory by delight.
With leafy pillows, bugs recline,
In a hammock woven of vine!

A turtle reads a book of jokes,
While ants parade in silly cloaks.
They chuckle loud, the breeze does tease,
What funny tales beneath the trees!

Lush Reverie

In my garden, gnomes do dance,
With tiny taps, they take a chance.
They sing of bugs and leafy wine,
While squirrels steal snacks, oh what a time!

The flowers gossip, petals wide,
About the snail who's got some pride.
He moves so slow, they can't believe,
In this race, he might just achieve!

A sunflower sways, a dance so grand,
It waves its head like a rock star band.
The bees keep buzzing, thinking it's jam,
But all they get is a flower's spam!

The grass tickles toes, a soft delight,
As frogs croak songs in the moonlight.
With every laugh, the night's anew,
In this laughing grove, there's mischief too!

Aisles of Illumination

At twilight's door, the fireflies greet,
They dance like lights on tiny feet.
The crickets chirp in silly beats,
Creating tunes where laughter meets.

A rabbit hops with grace so bold,
In moonlit aisles, he spins out gold.
While hedgehogs wear their knitted hats,
Debates on snacks—should they eat rats?

The mushrooms giggle, tops all bright,
They're plotting mischief for the night.
With every scoff from a passing toad,
A party starts, with joy bestowed!

In this bright land where critters play,
A nightly feast leads them astray.
With every laugh, they bridge the gloom,
In nature's hoot, there's always room!

The Secret of the Canopy

High above where owls reside,
They plot and plan for a night untied.
With whispers soft like a feather's touch,
They joke about things that matter much.

A squirrel's tale, absurd but spry,
Of acorn theft and a fruit pie.
They laugh aloud 'til the branches sway,
In leafy shadows, they jest and play.

Mossy nooks hold secrets deep,
In every fiber, laughter can seep.
The birds join in with chirps of glee,
Sharing delights of their grand jubilee.

So if you wander where the branches weave,
Listen close, and you might believe.
In bushes and boughs, hilarity thrives,
In each rustle, nature's laughter arrives!

The Glow of Nature's Heart

In twilight's blush, the trees do grin,
With glowing cores that burst within.
A brook babbles jokes of old,
Where leaves wink at tales oft retold.

The raccoons gather, wearing shades,
Their midnight meetings, grand charades.
With giggles echoing through the dark,
They plan the heist of the glowing spark.

The vines twist up in a silly dance,
Creating shadows that tease and prance.
While nocturnal critters cheer and race,
Each playful heart finds its own space.

So wander through this lively scene,
Where every glimmer feels like a dream.
In nature's laughter, we find our way,
With whimsy wrapped in night's bouquet!

Veils of Forest Light

In a forest thick and bright,
The squirrels play with all their might.
One stole my snack, what a cheek!
I'll get it back, I'll sneak and peek.

A glowworm dances with a glee,
Winking at an old, wise tree.
"Can you keep a secret dear?"
"Sure!" I said, but I couldn't hear!

The mushrooms giggle on the ground,
As ferns sway in the breeze around.
A rabbit hops in silly ways,
While other critters cheer and play.

Beneath the shafts of playful light,
I found a toad—what a sight!
He croaked a song of joy and fun,
And soon I joined; we danced as one.

Mossy Recollections

Sitting on a mossy patch,
I watched a bug try to catch
A leaf—it flipped and did a spin,
Then proudly claimed his silly win!

A snail with style slid on by,
With shades and swagger, oh my, oh my!
He winked at me, a suave old chap,
"Today I'll nap; how about a clap?"

The stories whispered in the breeze,
Of how a worm climbed up with ease.
He claimed the world was all his own,
While dancing on a toadstool throne.

In this lush grove, laughter blooms,
As every creature finds their tunes.
So join the fun, don't be a bore,
In nature's jest, we all explore!

Secrets of the Canopy

High above, the branches sway,
With secrets told in a light ballet.
A bird paused, then let out a laugh,
"Who knew a leaf could dance like that?"

A cheeky squirrel took a dive,
From branch to branch, he felt so alive!
He stashed his acorn with a grin,
Then poof! In fog, he blurred the din.

The shadows giggled, blending slow,
While little sprites put on a show.
With twinkling eyes and tender hearts,
They painted joy with leafy arts.

Amidst this whimsical parade,
I tripped on roots; oh what a stayed!
Yet laughter floated on the breeze,
As trees whispered, "Join us, please!"

Luminescent Whispers

At twilight's hour, the glow begins,
With fireflies buzzing like old friends.
A light so bright, it made me giggle,
They danced about like they're on a wiggle.

A hedgehog rolled, sporting a light,
"Look at me, I'm a star tonight!"
He twirled and spun on his little feet,
While all around, the critters beat.

Beneath the stars, the shadows creep,
With chuckles low, they lie in sleep.
But not before they share a jest,
About the lion who thought he's the best.

In this soft glow, we laugh and play,
As creatures join both night and day.
So here we gather, all aglow,
In the forest where the laughter flows.

Illuminated Paths of Nature's Canvas

Through the woods, a twinkle bright,
A squirrel wears a hat of light.
With every step, the shadows play,
Is that a fox? No, just some hay!

Beneath the trees, the fairies dance,
In clogs so big, they prance and prance.
A chorus of crickets starts to sing,
Is this the party? Bring your bling!

A rabbit hops with oversized shoes,
And joins the game, we're all big fools.
With every glow, a giggle bursts,
In nature's laugh, we quench our thirst!

As night wraps up its velvet cloak,
We share our tales, each one a joke.
In luminous hues, our dreams collide,
With nature's brush, we take wild rides.

The Soft Glow of Sylvan Secrets

In a glen where whispers play,
A turtle tells jokes, hip-hip-hooray!
With every chuckle, the fireflies wink,
"Is that my mom?" a bird takes a blink.

Mossy cushions, oh what a sight,
The raccoons have a pillow fight!
While owls hoot in a rhythmic cheer,
"Who's winning?" asks the hedgehog near.

The stream giggles, what a tease,
As pebbles dance in the midnight breeze.
Secrets of night, in whispers spun,
Nature's laughter, oh what fun!

The glow of hues, a secret land,
Where each creature has a quirky stand.
In moonlit corners, wrongs become right,
While we laugh together in the soft light.

Melodies of the Green-Hued Night

Beneath the glow, the frogs compose,
A symphony that tickles our toes.
With every ribbit, the night's a stage,
As otters join in, uncage the rage!

A dance-off leads by a pond so clear,
Where dragonflies spin without a fear.
With crickets strumming on leafy guitars,
The owls keep time, oh how they are stars!

A turtle breaks out in a jig quite bold,
Shaking his shell like it's bright gold.
Together we hum in the cool night air,
As starlight twinkles, joy everywhere.

In rhythms of laughter, darkness is bright,
Nature's band plays til the morning's light.
With every note, the night takes flight,
In this symphony of funny delight.

Nature's Lanterns in the Thicket

In thick bushes, lanterns grow,
Each one flickers, a cheeky show.
A raccoon struts, with swagger so fine,
"Is this a festival?" says a porcupine.

Glowworms pull pranks as they glide,
Jumping on leaves, in joy they ride.
A party where none take a break,
With twinkling whispers, they laugh and shake.

A fox juggles mushrooms with flair,
While an old badger starts to swear.
"Can you keep it down? I'm trying to nap!"
In this wild vaudeville, no one's a sap.

Each flicker tells a tale or two,
Of mischief and joy and a warm, bright hue.
As nature's shenanigans unfold and play,
We chuckle and cheer for another funny day!

Nature's Emerald Veil

In the woods where ferns do dance,
A squirrel with a funny glance.
He wears a hat made of a leaf,
A fashion choice that's quite a beef.

With ladybugs that chirp and laugh,
They plot to steal a rabbit's path.
A gnome's misplaced gardening tools,
Make them rivals like silly fools.

The trees all whisper silly jokes,
While mushrooms form a band of folks.
They play the tunes of crickets loud,
Amidst the laughter of the crowd.

A fox attempts a waltz so grand,
But ends up tripping on the land.
He poses like he meant to fall,
And shares a giggle with us all.

The Veil of Verdant Shadows

In leafy rooms where shadows play,
A frog prances with things to say.
He croaks a tune, a silly rhyme,
And claims it's worth a dime each time.

The owls wear glasses to look wise,
Confusing them with funny pies.
They blink and look for morning light,
While squirrels chuckle at their plight.

The butterflies hold court on blooms,
While ants march in odd little rooms.
They debate about the best snacks,
As bees just buzz and claim their hacks.

Amidst the green, the laughter swells,
Each creature shares their funny tales.
The jokes the trees would like to share,
Are hidden deep in leafy hair.

A Tapestry of Green Light

In the glen where shadows stretch and sway,
A rabbit hops in a charming way.
With polka dots upon his coat,
He dreams of sailing on a boat.

The thorns and thistles start to dance,
While snails take part in a slow prance.
They laugh and slip on drops of dew,
Their slippery steps, a funny view.

A turtle wearing shades of gold,
Shares stories of adventures bold.
His friends all chuckle at his tales,
As lizards join with tiny scales.

The breeze spreads giggles through the trees,
While branches sway like laughter's tease.
Each leaf a hat, each twig a wand,
In this green realm where fun responds.

The Forest's Gentle Caress

The woods are filled with silly sights,
As hedgehogs don their winter tights.
They roll around like awkward balls,
Embracing nature's gentle calls.

In a corner, mushrooms play charades,
While crickets join with funny braids.
Their games get tangled in the grass,
As squirrels watch with a laughing gasp.

A bear attempts to dance, oh dear!
His two left feet cause quite a cheer.
The rabbits giggle, point and jest,
While he just tries to do his best.

With giggles filling every nook,
The forest thrives on every look.
A symphony of nature's cheer,
In this green place, all is clear!

Secrets of the Shade

In the boughs a squirrel's hoot,
Wearing acorns like a suit.
The rabbits twitch their nose with glee,
While I pretend to sip my tea.

The shadows whisper silly tales,
Of haughty frogs and dancing snails.
A wise old owl gives a wink,
As I reconsider what I think.

A hedgehog juggles mushrooms bright,
While fireflies party late at night.
In this haven of absurd delight,
I lose my mind and take to flight.

The trees giggle in the breeze,
As I stumble over roots with ease.
And all the bushes start to sway,
When I burst forth with my ballet!

The Gentle Glow of Wilderness

The glowbugs have their evening show,
With costumes made from bits of glow.
In night's soft hue, I trip and yell,
My shadow seems to cast a spell!

A deer nearby gives me a stare,
Wondering why I dance in air.
The crickets join with jest and cheer,
As I attempt a swan dive here.

A raccoon steals a shiny treat,
While I dance with two left feet.
And in a quiet little sway,
I hear the trees start to replay!

The moon laughs softly from afar,
As I try to reach the stars.
In this wild, enchanted night,
Every blunder feels so right!

Legend of the Verdant Haven

There's a legend of a place quite green,
Where squirrels think they're royalty seen.
They throw acorn balls with a grin,
With thrones made of twigs piled high within.

The bunnies play a game of tag,
While I wiggle like a silly rag.
The trees keep score, and small birds cheer,
As I bumble in my best frontier!

A chattering chipmunk starts to sing,
Of the best belly flop contest in spring.
I try my hand, with no grace at all,
Splashing mud -- oh, what a call!

In this haven where laughter's alive,
Every giggle helps me thrive.
As leaves applaud my silly might,
I dance on until the morning light.

The Dance of Light and Leaf

The sun peeks through with a wink so sly,
I twirl like a leaf, oh so spry!
In the glimmering glow, I chance a fall,
With nature laughing, I just enthrall.

Butterflies come for the comedy show,
While ants line up in a neat row.
They clap their hands, oh what a sight,
As I trip again, a true delight!

With shadows playing tag in the sun,
The giggles chase me, what a run!
In this joyous, leafy ballet,
I forget my worries, hip hip hooray!

The wind whistles a cheeky tune,
Making me dance 'neath the smile of the moon.
And as the dusk envelopes the grove,
I'm the silly dancer the woods have known.

Secrets of the Enchanted Grove

In the woods where oddities dance,
Squirrels wear hats, and rabbits prance.
They hold tea parties on mushroom caps,
While raccoons trade snacks and share maps.

A wise old owl teaches the moon,
How to dance to a comical tune.
With rhythm of branches, they sway with glee,
As fireflies giggle, just to see.

Emerald Echoes of Forgotten Dreams

The frogs croak jokes from lily pads,
Telling tales that make you glad.
A turtle races, oh what a sight!
He's wearing sneakers, quite a delight.

Butterflies gossip about the breeze,
Teasing the flowers with playful tease.
A bumblebee buzzes with vibrant flair,
Says, "Have you heard? It's debonair!"

Lush Reveries in Dappled Shade

In this glen, the shadows play,
Tickling the leaves in a sneaky way.
A fox sneezes and starts a race,
While snickers echo in this serene space.

The sunbeams stretch, like cats at noon,
Chasing the clouds, they dance and swoon.
As laughter ripples through the air,
The trees join in, without a care.

The Glow of Moss-Covered Paths

Mossy green carpets underfoot,
Where giggling fairies take a snoot.
They trade silly secrets behind the bark,
While shadows play games, leaving their mark.

A hedgehog gets stuck in his own shell,
Thinking it's a cozy hotel.
But as that squirrel steals his snack,
He chuckles softly, with a little quack.

Whimsy Beneath the Forest's Glow

In shades of green, the squirrels prance,
With acorns bouncing in a dance.
The rabbits hop in silly circles,
While frogs debate in tiny sparkles.

A bear tries to balance on a log,
But slips and makes it quite the slog.
The owls hoot in muffled fits,
As all the forest giggles in bits.

The mushrooms wear their finest hats,
Inviting in the passing rats.
Chipmunks join with tiny cheers,
As the laughter echoes through the years.

Beneath the boughs, where mischief thrives,
The trees cradle the joking lives.
In every rustle, a joke that's told,
A rollicking tale of nature bold.

In the Embrace of Nature's Light

A sunbeam tickles the bushes wide,
As bees in tutus joyfully glide.
The daisies wear their sunny smiles,
While ants parade in perfect files.

A goat, a fool, on a grassy slope,
Tries to juggle apples, full of hope.
But whoops! One flies and hits a tree,
And all the critters laugh with glee.

The brook hums tunes to the bouncy beetles,
While frogs in sunglasses strum their fiddles.
In this bright dance of nature's cheer,
Every creature gathers near.

So let's rejoice in the comic view,
Of playful antics in the hue.
With every wink from leaf to light,
The forest sings through day and night.

Journeys through the Emerald Abyss

A turtle dons his travel hat,
And begs the snail to join the chat.
Together through the ferns they roam,
But both are slow to find their home.

The lizards giggle up the trees,
As they slip down with unexpected ease.
Chasing shadows in the sun's embrace,
They race with grace in a funny chase.

A hedgehog rolls, a tiny ball,
While birds above just watch it fall.
The path ahead is quite unclear,
But laughter leads them, never fear.

In emerald hues, their cares are shed,
With every laugh, new dreams are spread.
Adventure waits in every nook,
Nature's book is filled with charm and hook.

Flickers of Faerie Light in the Woods

At twilight's hush, the lights appear,
Tiny faeries giggle in their cheer.
They twirl and dance on leaves so bright,
Each flash a wink, a funny sight.

The toadstools play a game of hide,
While fireflies take a frantic ride.
Hopping here and flitting there,
Making mischief without a care.

A raccoon tries to join the fun,
Though tangled up, he's come undone.
With each misstep, the giggles rise,
As he tumbles down, what a surprise!

Each spark and flicker holds a jest,
In this wood, their wise hearts rest.
For laughter's found in every flight,
In nature's warmth, everything feels right.

When Ferns Speak in Luminescence

In a forest where ferns giggle,
Mossy beds play tag with the light.
Sassy sprites give a wiggle,
While toads croak with delight.

The shadows seem to dance,
In a play of chase and run.
Ferns wear their best green pants,
As elves join in the fun!

A squirrel rides a dragonfly,
Making all the critters cheer.
Underneath a winking sky,
They share stories, full of cheer.

As night wraps its cozy arm,
The fireflies join the scene.
With laughter and harmless charm,
The woods feel like a dream.

Twilight in the Forest's Heart

When twilight brings a giggly tune,
Owl's wise cracks light the air.
Frogs croon like they're on the moon,
While raccoons just stop and stare.

Mushrooms march in silly rows,
With hats that sing and swirl.
They dance as if no one knows,
In shades of pink and pearl.

A critter band strikes up a beat,
With acorns clapping loud.
Jays jazz up with wings so fleet,
Creating quite the crowd!

As night settles, laughter stays,
Enchanted by the spark.
The forest plays its funny plays,
In the glow of twilight's mark.

A Prism through the Canopy

Through a prism of light so bright,
Squirrels sparkle in their prance.
Kangaroo mice hop with delight,
In a frolicsome forest dance.

The branches whisper ancient jokes,
That tickle the mossy floor.
All the silly little folks,
Can't help but laugh and roar!

Brilliant hues play peek-a-boo,
As butterflies flit and glide.
Silly shadows form a queue,
And in giggles, all abide.

In that vibrant, bustling glen,
Life laughs with a twinkling eye.
Where every fleeting moment's then,
A reason to dance and fly.

Glimmers of Life in the Woodland

In the woodland where glimmers gleam,
A hedgehog tries to juggle night.
With acorns, it's an absurd dream,
It fumbles, creating quite a sight.

The bushes hum a merry tune,
While creatures tap their furry feet.
Fireflies blink like mini moons,
As night unfolds its playful sheet.

Bunnies bounce in bright delight,
Wiggling noses, feeling spry.
The breeze brings tales of light,
With whispers of a friendly sigh.

Laughter echoes through the trees,
As mischief reigns in every nook.
In a world where fun is key,
The woodland writes its charming book.

Heartbeat of the Grove

In the wood where squirrels dance,
They always seem to take a chance.
A bird with a hat sings a tune,
While rabbits debate the best time for noon.

The trees wear socks, oh what a sight,
With lightning bugs buzzing left and right.
A chipmunk's joke makes the leaves all shake,
As old oaks gossip about last twirl's mistake.

Mushrooms in bow ties dance through the fog,
While frogs recite poetry, sounding like a dog.
A shy tree stump joins in on the fun,
Together they laugh, till the day is done.

Nature's critters hold a grand parade,
With ants in pants, dancing unafraid.
In this grove, laughter calls the day,
Let's all rejoice, hip-hip-hooray!

Nature's Shimmering Cloak

In a glade where shadows play tricks,
The flowers burst out in giggly kicks.
A daisy dons glasses, a bumblebee cap,
While daisies narrate tales of a nap.

The creek tickles minnows as they swim,
While frogs in tuxedos sing loud and prim.
A napping bear snores, then wakes with a howl,
Scares the fish who were in for a stroll.

The sun paints the leaves in wacky hues,
As snails slide by with glittery shoes.
Vines twist around for a wild little dance,
While trees tap their roots as if in a trance.

In this cloak of fun, the animals thrive,
Practicing their moves, keeping dreams alive.
They'll twirl under starlight, rejoice far and wide,
Celebrating nature with sprightly pride!

Enchanted Paths in Green Light

Down winding trails where laughter is found,
The flowers tell secrets, the grass is unbound.
A sneaky fox wears a shiny bow tie,
As butterflies chuckle and hop up on high.

Gnomes play poker beneath the tall ferns,
They wager their hats and giggle, it churns.
With the sun in their eyes and mischief at play,
They sing silly ballads to brighten up the day.

The breeze carries whispers; the crickets say woo,
A hedgehog tells stories, and they all go "moo!"
A squirrel's puppet show brings cheers from the crowd,
As the audience squeals and jumps all around.

In this realm of whimsy, the joy never halts,
With laughter and friendship, life's just a waltz.
Each step is a joke, every turn's a surprise,
In paths filled with wonder, we dance 'neath the skies.

The Illumination of Flora

In a garden where giggles blossom with cheer,
The daisies prick up when the sun is near.
Bees swap gossip over honeyed tea,
While petals all share their wild fantasy.

A sunflower wears shades to keep things bright,
While busy bees buzz in a quirky flight.
The tulips gossip, sharing silly charms,
Enticing the breeze into their flowered arms.

The carrots all jiggle in their earthy beds,
As beetles play chess on top of their heads.
Tomatoes are blushing, all shy in the sun,
While the dew drops chuckle, having too much fun.

In this show of colors, whimsy takes flight,
The flora's bright laughter dances through the night.
With each quirky bloom, a new tale ignites,
And the garden hums joy under soft twinkling lights.

Serene Light Beneath Branches

In the forest, a squirrel sneezed,
A leaf fell down, unplanned and teased.
The sun giggled, shining bright,
As shadows danced with sheer delight.

A bunny wore a tiny hat,
Chasing whispers from a chat.
The flowers swayed, all turned around,
As laughter echoed all around.

A raccoon played a silly tune,
With a stick that looked like a croon.
The trees applauded with a rustle,
While critters joined in a joyful hustle.

In this place where chuckles reign,
Nature's mischief, never plain.
Beneath the branches, joy will bloom,
In the forest's waistband of green gloom.

The Soft Embrace of Nature

A frog in a coat sang with flair,
Challenged the wind to a fair.
Grass tickled the toes of a snickering hare,
As bees buzzed jokes without a care.

A chubby bear danced, oh so spry,
With honey pots, he did fly.
The sun chuckled from way up high,
While birds chimed in, singing "Oh my!"

Leaves rustled boldly, sharing a jest,
While ants played hide and seek in their nest.
Under the sun's grin, shadows confide,
Nature's wittiness, a sweet ride.

Mushrooms helped a snail with a scare,
"Don't worry, we're not going anywhere!"
In this frolic, laughter's the goal,
Every creature plays its humorous role.

Beneath the Boughs

A porcupine wore a fancy tie,
While birds in wigs went flitting by.
Nutty jokes passed between the trees,
And grasshoppers laughed with such ease.

A turtle tried to race a snail,
While fireflies told tales without fail.
The moon peeked through to join in the play,
As shadows twinkled, brightening the way.

Rabbits played hopscotch, hopping high,
While owls guessed riddles, oh my, oh my!
Each leaf a witness to silly dreams,
As the night giggled with soft moonbeams.

In this world, every heart is light,
With whispers of joy that take flight.
Beneath these branches of stories bold,
A comedic tale in green unfolds.

Sylvan Enchantment

A hedgehog tried to juggle pinecones,
While chipmunks cheered with happy tones.
The breeze floated in with tickling charms,
Wrapping each critter in nature's arms.

Beneath the fern's playful gaze,
Ants held parades in a merry craze.
Singing to flowers, a tune so sweet,
While beetles served snacks, a delightful treat.

The owls cracked jokes, wise and bold,
As daylight teased the stories told.
Each tiny creature donned a grin,
In this forest, laughter's the win.

Even daffodils danced with glee,
Rooted in fun, as happy as can be.
A soft enchantment we embrace,
In this lovely, silly green space.

Beneath the Verdant Whisperings

In the forest where the frogs do croak,
The trees giggle, they've told a joke.
Squirrels dance with acorn hats,
While foxes laugh at sleepy cats.

Beneath the leaves, a rabbit sings,
Wearing shades like funky kings.
The sunbeam tickles each twig and branch,
Join the critters for a silly dance.

The mushrooms sport their polka dots,
And everyone has funny thoughts.
Bouncing carrots jump with glee,
It's the wildest, wackiest jamboree!

So grab your friends and come along,
In the woods, where we all belong.
With laughter echoing, hearts so bright,
We'll dance till day gives way to night.

Journey through Light-Infused Foliage.

A chase begins with shadows near,
As butterflies giggle, never fear.
With wobbly legs and flapping wings,
Chasing sunbeams, oh what fun it brings!

The owls wear glasses, wise and round,
While chubby chipmunks scoot around.
Each winding path a merry surprise,
With laughter bubbling to the skies.

Pinecones tumble like comical stars,
Racing down, they've come from Mars!
The ground is soft with mossy beds,
Come join the fun, don't use your heads!

So merrily hum as you skip along,
In the canopy where you belong.
With giggles and joy, let's roam the day,
In light-infused foliage, let's play away!

Luminescent Canopy

Beneath bright lights, the trees take flight,
They sway and twist, feeling quite right.
Among the branches, a party is found,
With fireflies buzzing and laughter all around.

A dancing frog is the star of the show,
With moves so silly, it steals the glow.
Acorns applaud with a clink and a clank,
In a feathery hat, our frog gives a prank!

The raccoons serve snacks, all mixed and strange,
With broccoli cakes, how very deranged!
Squeaky squeals of delight fill the air,
As cheeky chipmunks roll without a care.

So come take a seat on a luminous log,
Join the giggles with each happy frog.
In the canopy, let's share the cheer,
In this wild party, there's nothing to fear!

Whispers in the Shade

In the shade where whispers dwell,
The giggles bounce, oh can't you tell?
A hedgehog juggles while spinning around,
With a harmony of chuckles, a delightful sound.

The shadows play hide-and-seek with the sun,
As round mushrooms spin just for fun.
A tiny worm draws doodles on leaves,
Creating masterpieces, oh how one believes!

With every rustle, a story unfolds,
Of silly pranks and treasures untold.
The crickets chirp their curious tunes,
As the flowers dance beneath the moon.

So let's relax in this laughter parade,
Where every corner holds a charm made.
With every giggle, the world's more bright,
In the shade, we'll savor pure delight!

Nature's Ethereal Embrace

In the woods, a squirrel prances,
Chasing shadows, taking chances.
With acorn hats and nutty schemes,
They play like actors in wild dreams.

The mushrooms wear their spotted hats,
Conspiring with the sneaky rats.
Together they throw a garden ball,
Where flowers dance and twigs enthrall.

A rabbit juggles dandelions,
To entertain the alignin' lions.
The deer laugh with a twinkling eye,
As frogs try to hop, but just fly by.

So come and join this jolly spree,
Where nature's jokes run wild and free.
In every leaf, a giggle glows,
In nature's arms, the laughter flows.

A Symphony of Green Light

A parrot sings, a silly tune,
Bouncing high like a tiny balloon.
The crickets tap their tiny feet,
Creating rhythms that can't be beat.

The ants march by in perfect rows,
Carrying snacks beneath their toes.
With pie and cake made of pure mud,
They feast like kings in the green flood.

Bees buzz with a raucous cheer,
Throwing shade with their tiny beer.
While flowers blush, they shimmy and sway,
Singing loud to greet the day.

So let us dance in this wild parade,
Where every swing comes with a shade.
In nature's tune, we sing so bright,
In a symphony of sheer delight.

Tales of the Lush Wilderness

In a thicket lurks a curious fox,
Wearing shades and glittering socks.
He tells tall tales of daring deeds,
Of races with the nimble weeds.

The owls convene for a late-night chat,
Discussing life, while swinging flat.
With glowing eyes and feathered hats,
They spill their secrets like chubby cats.

A turtle turns to disco craze,
Shrugging off the classic ways.
With every spin, they giggle loud,
Drawing in an amazed crowd.

So grab your snacks and join their fun,
Chasing shadows till the day is done.
In tales spun wild beneath the trees,
Find laughter carried on the breeze.

The Gentle Touch of Flora

The daisies chuckle, displaying cheer,
As dandelions blow, spreading cheer.
With petals soft as feathery dreams,
They plot mischief in sunlit beams.

A cactus dons a feather boa,
Trying to dance to the flow of a showa.
While violets giggle by the stream,
Mapping out their garden dream.

Sunflowers sway in breezy delight,
Arranging gossip that's far from polite.
"Did you see that worm? What a silly sight!"
They croon to the moon, still glowing bright.

So join the fun where nature thrives,
In every flower, a laugh survives.
With every petal, a story spins,
In this floral dance where joy begins.

www.ingramcontent.com/pod-product-compliance
Lightning Source LLC
Chambersburg PA
CBHW070305120526
44590CB00017B/2569